Congressional Research Service

Latin America: Terrorism Issues

Mark P. Sullivan
Specialist in Latin American Affairs

March 2, 2012

Congressional Research Service

7-5700

www.crs.gov

RS21049

CRS Report for Congress ───────────
Prepared for Members and Committees of Congress

Summary

U.S. attention to terrorism in Latin America intensified in the aftermath of the September 2001 terrorist attacks on New York and Washington, with an increase in bilateral and regional cooperation. In its 2010 Country Reports on Terrorism (issued in August 2011), the State Department maintained that terrorism in the region was primarily perpetrated by terrorist organizations in Colombia and by the remnants of radical leftist Andean groups. Overall, however, the report maintained that the threat of a transnational terrorist attack remained low for most countries in the hemisphere. With regard to concerns about drug trafficking-related violence in Mexico, the State Department terrorism report asserted that "there was no evidence of ties between Mexican criminal organizations and terrorist groups, nor that the criminal organizations had aims of political or territorial control, aside from seeking to protect and expand the impunity with which they conduct their criminal activity." Cuba has remained on the State Department's list of state sponsors of terrorism since 1982 pursuant to Section 6(j) of the Export Administration Act, which triggers a number of economic sanctions. Both Cuba and Venezuela are on the State Department's annual list of countries determined to be not cooperating fully with U.S. antiterrorism efforts pursuant to Section 40A of the Arms Export Control Act. U.S. officials have expressed concerns over the past several years about Venezuela's lack of cooperation on antiterrorism efforts, its relations with Iran, and potential support for Colombian terrorist groups.

Over the past several years, policymakers have been concerned about Iran's increasing activities in Latin America, particularly its relations with Venezuela, although there has been disagreement over the extent and significance of Iran's relations with the region. Concerns center on Iran's attempts to circumvent U.N. and U.S. sanctions, as well as on its ties to the radical Lebanon-based Islamic group Hezbollah. Both Iran and Hezbollah are reported to be linked to two bombings against Jewish targets in Argentina in the early 1990s. The State Department terrorism report maintains that there are no known operational cells of either Al Qaeda or Hezbollah-related groups in the hemisphere, but noted that "ideological sympathizers in South America and the Caribbean continued to provide financial and moral support to these and other terrorist groups in the Middle East and South Asia."

In the 112th Congress, several initiatives have been introduced related to terrorism issues in the Western Hemisphere regarding Mexico, Venezuela, and the activities of Iran and Hezbollah, and several oversight hearings have been held. **H.R. 3401** (Mack), marked up by the House Subcommittee on the Western Hemisphere on December 15, 2011, would require the Secretary of State to submit a detailed counterinsurgency strategy "to combat the terrorist insurgency in Mexico waged by transnational criminal organizations." **H.R. 3783** (Duncan), amended and approved on March 1, 2012, by the House Foreign Affairs Committee's Subcommittee on Terrorism, Nonproliferation, and Trade would require the Administration to develop "a strategy to address Iran's growing hostile presence and activity in the Western Hemisphere." Among other introduced initiatives, **H.R. 1270** (McCaul) would direct the Secretary of State to designate as foreign terrorist organizations six Mexican drug cartels, and **H.Res. 247** (Mack) would call for the designation of Venezuela as a state sponsor of terrorism. (For further discussion of these bills, see "112th Congress" below.)

Contents

Figures

Contacts

Terrorism in Latin America: U.S. Concerns

Over the years, the United States has been concerned about threats to Latin American and Caribbean nations from various terrorist or insurgent groups that have attempted to influence or overthrow elected governments. Although Latin America has not been the focal point in the war on terrorism, countries in the region have struggled with domestic terrorism for decades and international terrorist groups have at times used the region as a battleground to advance their causes.

The State Department's annual *Country Reports on Terrorism* highlights U.S. concerns about terrorist threats around the world, including in Latin America. The 2010 report (issued in August 2011) maintained that terrorist attacks in the region were primarily perpetrated by terrorist organizations in Colombia and by the remnants of radical leftist Andean groups. Overall, however, the report maintained that the threat of a transnational terrorist attack remained low for most countries in the hemisphere. The report also asserted that there were no known operational cells of either Al Qaeda or Hezbollah-related groups in the hemisphere, but noted that "ideological sympathizers in South America and the Caribbean continued to provide financial and moral support to these and other terrorist groups in the Middle East and South Asia." With regard to concerns about rising drug trafficking-related violence in Mexico, the State Department report asserted that "there was no evidence of ties between Mexican criminal organizations and terrorist groups, nor that the criminal organizations had aims of political or territorial control, aside from seeking to protect and expand the impunity with which they conduct their criminal activity."[1]

The report also stated that regional governments "took modest steps to improve their counterterrorism capabilities and tighten border security" but that progress was limited by "corruption, weak government institutions, insufficient interagency cooperation, weak or non-existent legislation, and reluctance to allocate sufficient resources." The report singled out Argentina, Colombia, and Mexico for undertaking serious prevention and preparedness efforts, and noted that "most countries began to look seriously at possible connections between transnational criminal organizations and terrorist organizations." It also noted that most hemispheric nations had solid cooperation with the United States on terrorism issues, especially at the operational level, with excellent intelligence, law enforcement, and legal assistance relations. The report cited the Inter-American Committee Against Terrorism (CICTE) at the Organization of American States as important for U.S. cooperation on terrorism with the region.

The State Department currently lists two Latin American countries—Cuba and Venezuela—on its annual list of countries that are not "cooperating fully with United States antiterrorism efforts" pursuant to Section 40A of the Arms Export Control Act. The most recent annual determination was made in May 2011.[2] In addition, Cuba has been on the State Department's state sponsors of terrorism list pursuant to Section 6(j) of the Export Administration Act (EAA) of 1979 since 1982. The state sponsors of terrorism list is not an annual list. Rather, countries remain on the list until either the President or Congress takes action to remove a country. The EAA sets forth procedures for the President to remove a country from the list.

---

[1] U.S. Department of State, "Country Reports on Terrorism 2010," August 18, 2011, available at http://www.state.gov/s/ct/rls/crt/2010/index htm

[2] Department of State, "Determination and Certification Under Section 40A of the Arms Export Control Act," 76 *Federal Register* 31390, May 31, 2011.

Colombia

Colombia has three terrorist groups that have been designated by the Secretary of State as Foreign Terrorist Organizations (FTOs): the leftist National Liberation Army (ELN), remaining elements of the demobilized rightist paramilitary United Self-Defense Forces of Colombia (AUC), and the leftist Revolutionary Armed Forces of Colombia (FARC).

The ELN reportedly has a dwindling membership of about 1,250 fighters with diminished resources and reduced offensive capability, but has continued to inflict casualties through the use of land mines and ambushes and continues to fund its operations through drug trafficking, kidnapping, and extortion, according to the State Department's 2010 terrorism report. Past peace talks between the ELN and the Colombian government ended in 2008.

With more than 32,000 members demobilized, the AUC remained inactive as a formal organization, but some former AUC paramilitaries continued to engage in criminal activities, mostly drug trafficking, in newly emerging criminal organizations (known as BACRIM, *Bandas Criminales Emergentes*). Estimates of the membership of these BACRIM range from over 3,500 to 6,000 or more. According to the terrorism report, the Colombian government continued to process and investigate demobilized paramilitaries under the Justice and Peace Law, which offers judicial benefits and reduced prison sentences for participants who confess fully to their crimes and return all illicit profits. Many former AUC members also were receiving some reintegration benefits.

Over the past several years, the FARC has been weakened significantly by the government's military campaign against it, including the killings of several FARC commanders in 2007 and the group's second in command, Raúl Reyes, during a Colombian government raid on a FARC camp in Ecuador on March 1, 2008. In May 2008, the FARC admitted that its long-time leader, Manuel Marulanda, had died of a heart attack in March. In July 2008, a Colombian military operation in the southeastern province of Guaviare rescued 15 long-held hostages, including three U.S. defense contractors held since February 2003—Thomas Howes, Keith Stansell, and Marc Gonsalves; Colombian Senator and presidential candidate Ingrid Betancourt; and other Colombians. The Colombian military dealt a significant blow to the terrorist group in September 2010 when it killed a top military commander, Victor Julio Suárez (aka "Mono Joyoy") in a bombing raid on his camp in a mountainous region of Meta department in central Colombia. Even more significantly, in early November 2011, the Colombian military killed FARC leader Alfonso Cano in a bombing raid in the department of Cauca in southwestern Colombia. In the aftermath of Cano's death, Rodrigo Londoño, also known as Timoleón Jiménez or Timochenko, a long-time member of the FARC Secretariat, was chosen as the FARC's new leader in mid-November 2011.

The FARC is still estimated to have a strength of around 8,000, with the group responsible for terrorist attacks, extortion, and kidnappings. In late November 2011, the FARC executed four hostages who had been held for more than a decade when the Colombian military approached a guerrilla camp in the southern department of Caqueta.

Colombian terrorist groups continue to utilize territory of several of Colombia's neighbors— Ecuador, Panama, Peru, and Venezuela—according to the State Department's terrorism report (see **Figure 1**). The FARC has training and logistical supply camps along Ecuador's northern border with Colombia. While Ecuador's relations with Colombia became tense in the aftermath of Colombia's March 2008 military raid on a FARC camp in Ecuador's Sucumbios province, Ecuador's military subsequently increased the number of operations against the FARC in its northern border region. Nevertheless, according to the 2010 terrorism report, resource constraints and limited capabilities affected Ecuador's actions. Under new Colombian President Juan Manuel Santos, the two countries made progress in improving bilateral relations, and restored diplomatic relations in December 2010.

Figure 1. Colombia and Neighboring Countries

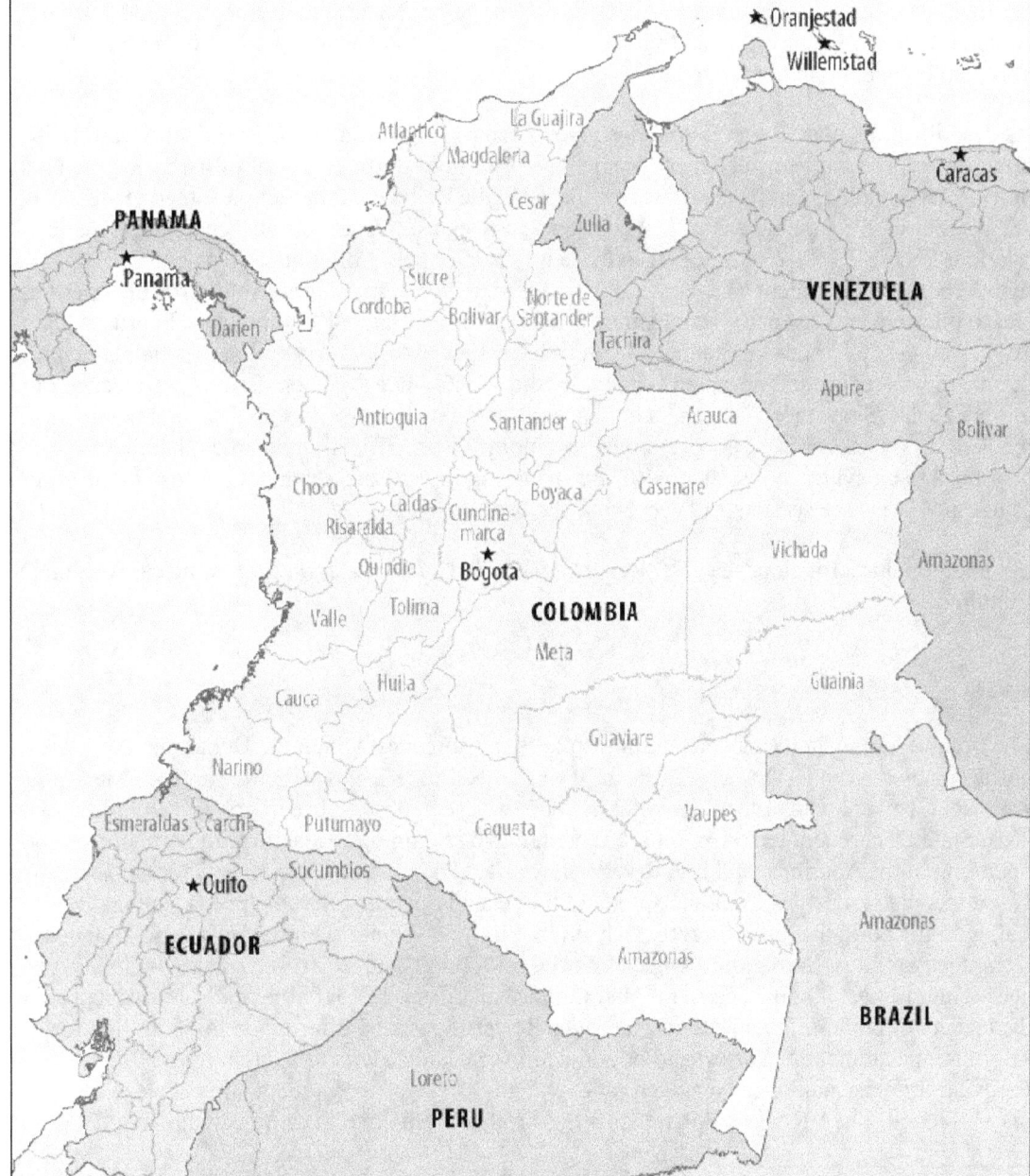

Source: CRS.

Notes: The map shows Colombia's departments and the bordering departments, provinces, and states of neighboring Ecuador, Peru, Brazil, Venezuela, and Panama.

In Panama, a small number of FARC members from the group's 57th Front were reported to operate in the country's Darien province bordering Colombia, using the area as a safe haven. In January 2010, three FARC members were killed and two were captured in a clash with Panamanian forces in Darien, while late in 2010, Panama and Colombia agreed to establish police stations near each side of the border.

In Peru, the FARC was reported to use remote areas along the Colombian-Peruvian border to rest, regroup, and make arms purchases. According to the State Department terrorism report, experts contend that the FARC continued to fund coca cultivation and cocaine production among the Peruvian population in border areas.

As described in the 2010 terrorism report, the Colombian government of President Alvaro Uribe publicly accused the Venezuelan government several times during the year of harboring members of the FARC and ELN in its territory. In July 2010, the Uribe government presented evidence at the OAS of FARC training camps in Venezuela. In response, Venezuela suspended diplomatic relations on July 22, 2010, yet less than three weeks later new Colombian President Santos met with Venezuelan President Chávez and the two leaders agreed to reestablish diplomatic relations and to improve military patrols along their border. In congressional testimony on February 15, 2011, Assistant Secretary of State for Western Hemisphere Affairs Arturo Valenzuela maintained that there was reduced Venezuelan support for the FARC since President Santos has reached out to Venezuela.[3] Since then, Venezuela has captured and returned to Colombia several members of the FARC. In October 2011 congressional testimony, a U.S. official maintained that there continues to be evidence that the FARC are sheltering in Venezuela, but not as close to the border as before.[4] (Also see section on "Venezuela" below.)

For additional information, see CRS Report RL32250, *Colombia: Issues for Congress*, by June S. Beittel.

Peru

The brutal Shining Path (Sendero Luminoso or SL) insurgency, which the Department of State has designated as an FTO, was significantly weakened in the 1990s with the capture of its leader Abimael Guzman, who, after a new trial in 2006, was sentenced to life in prison. According to the 2010 State Department terrorism report, there are two remaining SL factions in Peru, one operating in the Apurimac and Ene River Valley (VRAE) in the south led by Victor Quispe Palomino, also known as Comrade José, and the second operating in the Upper Huallaga River Valley in the north that until recently was led by Florindo Eleuterio Flores Hala (also known as Comrade Artemio). Both groups engage in drug trafficking, and in 2010 carried out 136 terrorist acts, with killings of police, civilians, and military members. In 2010, the State Department added the leaders of both SL factions to its Narcotics Reward Program, offering up to $5 million for information leading to the arrest and/or conviction of each leader. On February 12, 2012, Peruvian officials announced that Comrade Artemio had been captured, dealing a heavy blow to his SL faction. The VRAE faction remains the stronger of the two SL groups, with about 300

---

[3] "House Foreign Affairs Subcommittee on Western Hemisphere Holds Hearing on U.S.-Latin America Relations," *CQ Congressional Transcripts*, February 15, 2011.

[4] See testimony of Kevin Whitaker, Deputy Assistant Secretary of State for Western Hemisphere Affairs in "The Senate Caucus on International Narcotics Control Holds a Hearing on 'U.S.-Andean Security Cooperation,'—News Event," *Political Transcripts by CQ Transcriptions*, October 19, 2011.

members compared to about 100 members of the Upper Huallaga River Valley faction at the time of Artemio's capture.[5] (Also see discussion above on the FARC's activities in border areas with Colombia.)

Cuba

The Department of State, pursuant to Section 6(j) of the Export Administration Act (EAA) of 1979, has included Cuba among its list of states sponsoring terrorism since 1982 (the other states currently on the list are Iran, Sudan, and Syria). Communist Cuba had a history of supporting revolutionary movements and governments in Latin America and Africa, but in 1992, then Cuban leader Fidel Castro said that his country's support for insurgents abroad was a thing of the past. Most analysts accept that Cuba's policy generally did change, largely because the breakup of the Soviet Union resulted in the loss of billions in subsidies.

The State Department's 2010 terrorism report (issued in August 2011) stated that the Cuban government "maintained a public stance against terrorism and terrorist financing, but there was no evidence that it had severed ties with elements from the Revolutionary Armed Forces of Colombia (FARC) and recent media reports indicate some current and former members of the Basque Fatherland and Liberty (ETA) continue to reside in Cuba." The report further stated that "available information suggested that the Cuban government maintained limited contact with FARC members, but there was no evidence of direct financial or ongoing material support." It maintained that Cuba allowed Spanish police to travel to Cuba to confirm the presence of suspected ETA members. As in previous years, the report maintained that Cuba continued to denounce U.S. counterterrorism efforts worldwide.

The 2010 terrorism report also maintained that Cuba has been used as a transit point by third-country nationals to enter the United States illegally, and that Cuba was aware of the concerns posed by such threats and took action to investigate third country migrant smuggling and related criminal activities. The report noted that the Cuban government allowed representatives of the U.S. Transportation Security Administration to conduct a series of airport security visits throughout the country in November 2010.

Cuba's retention on the terrorism list has been questioned by some observers. In general, those who support keeping Cuba on the list point to the government's history of supporting terrorist acts and armed insurgencies in Latin America and Africa. They point to the government's continued hosting of members of foreign terrorist organizations and U.S. fugitives from justice. Critics of retaining Cuba on the terrorism list maintain that it is a holdover of the Cold War. They argue that domestic political considerations keep Cuba on the terrorism list, while North Korea and Libya (before the overthrow of the Qadhafi regime) were removed, and maintain that Cuba's presence on the list diverts U.S. attention from struggles against serious terrorist threats.

Both the President and Congress have powers to take a country off the state sponsors of terrorism list. As set forth in Section 6(j) of the Export Administration Act, a country's retention on the list may be rescinded in two ways. The first option is for the President to submit a report to Congress certifying that there has been a fundamental change in the leadership and policies of the government and that the government is not supporting acts of international terrorism and is

---

[5] "Capture of 'Artemio' Heralds New Phase in Peruvian Insurgency," Latin News Daily Report, February 22, 2012; "Peru Politics: Remnants of Shining Path on the Run," *Economist Intelligence Unit ViewsWire*, February 23, 2012.

providing assurances that it will not support such acts in the future. The second option is for the President to submit a report to Congress, at least 45 days in advance justifying the rescission and certifying that the government has not provided any support for international terrorism during the preceding six months, and has provided assurances that it will not support such acts in the future. If Congress disagrees with the President's decision to remove a country from the list, it could seek to block the rescission through legislation.

Congress also has the power on its own to remove a country from the terrorism list. For example, legislation introduced on Cuba in the 111th Congress, H.R. 2272 (Rush), included a provision that would have rescinded the Secretary of State's determination that Cuba "has repeatedly provided support for acts of international terrorism."

Cuba has been the target of various terrorist incidents over the years. In 1976, a Cuban plane was bombed, killing 73 people. In 1997, there were almost a dozen bombings in the tourist sector in Havana in which an Italian businessman was killed and several others were injured. Two Salvadorans were convicted and sentenced to death for the 1997 bombings in March 1999 (although the sentences were commuted in 2010 to 30 years in prison), and three Guatemalans were sentenced to prison terms ranging from 10 to 15 years in January 2002 for plans to conduct bombings in 1998. In December 2010, another Salvadoran, Francisco Chávez Abarca, was convicted for involvement in the 1997 bombings in Havana and sentenced to 30 years in prison.

In November 2000, four anti-Castro activists were arrested in Panama for a plot to kill Fidel Castro. One of the accused, Luis Posada Carriles, is also alleged to be involved in the 1976 Cuban airline bombing and the series of bombings in Havana in 1997 noted above.[6] The four stood trial in March 2004 and were sentenced on weapons charges to prison terms ranging from seven to eight years. In late August 2004, Panamanian President Mireya Moscoso pardoned the four men before the end of her presidential term.

Posada entered the United States illegally in 2005. In subsequent removal proceedings, an immigration judge found that Posada could not be removed to Cuba or Venezuela because of concerns that he would face torture, and he was thereafter permitted to remain in the United States pending such time as he could be transferred to a different country. Posada subsequently applied for naturalization to become a U.S. citizen. This application was denied, and criminal charges were brought against him for allegedly false statements made in his naturalization application and interview. Although a federal district court dismissed the indictment in 2007, its ruling was reversed by an appellate court in 2008. In April 2009, the United States filed a superseding indictment, which included additional criminal charges based on allegedly false statements made by Posada in immigration removal proceedings concerning his involvement in the 1997 Havana bombings. His trial originally was set to begin in August 2009, but was rescheduled three times until it finally began in January 2011.[7] Ultimately, Posada was acquitted of the perjury charges in April 2011, an action that was strongly criticized by Cuban officials.

---

[6] Frances Robles, "An Old Foe of Castro Looks Back on His Fight," *Miami Herald*, September 4, 2003.

[7] For additional information, see "Background on Luis Posada Carriles," CRS Congressional Distribution Memorandum, December 8, 2010, prepared by Mark P. Sullivan, Specialist in Latin American Affairs, and Michael John Garcia, Legislative Attorney. Available from the authors.

For additional information on Cuba, see CRS Report R41617, *Cuba: Issues for the 112ᵗʰ Congress*. For background, see CRS Report RL32251, *Cuba and the State Sponsors of Terrorism List*.

Venezuela[8]

U.S. officials have expressed concerns over the past several years about Venezuela's lack of cooperation on antiterrorism efforts, President Hugo Chávez's sympathetic statements for Colombian terrorist groups, and Venezuela's relations with Iran. Since May 2006, the Secretary of State has made an annual determination that Venezuela has not been "cooperating fully with United States antiterrorism efforts" pursuant to Section 40A of the Arms Export Control Act (AECA). The most recent determination was made in May 2011. As a result, the United States imposed an arms embargo on Venezuela in 2006, which ended all U.S. commercial arms sales and retransfers to Venezuela. (Other countries currently on the Section 40A list include Cuba, Eritrea, Iran, North Korea, and Syria, not to be confused with the "state sponsors of terrorism" list under Section 6(j) of the Export Administration Act of 1979.) In June 2011 congressional testimony, State Department officials again expressed concern about "Venezuela's relations with Iran, its support for the FARC, [and] its lackluster cooperation on counterterrorism."[9]

In its 2010 terrorism report (issued in August 2011), the State Department maintained that the Venezuelan government took no action against Venezuelan government and military officials linked to the FARC and ELN, Colombia's two guerrilla insurgent groups. While it described Colombia's accusations against the Venezuelan government for harboring the FARC and ELN, the report also noted an improved bilateral Colombian-Venezuelan relationship on security issues under the new government of Colombian President Juan Manuel Santos, including Venezuela's extradition to Colombia of several suspected members of the terrorists groups.

According to June 2011 State Department congressional testimony, "Colombian-Venezuelan cooperation on terrorism and security matters is clearly increasing and being systematized, yielding notable results." The State Department noted Venezuela's deportation of several FARC and ELN members to Colombia, including key operatives and high-profile political actors. It said that President Chávez has "called on the FARC to join a political reconciliation process and has claimed that any discussion between Venezuelan government officials and the FARC about establishing bases in Venezuela took place without his authorization."[10] As discussed above, a U.S. official testified in October 2011 there continues to be evidence that the FARC are sheltering in Venezuela, but not as close to the border as before. (See "Colombia" above.)

---

[8] For additional background on Venezuela, see CRS Report R40938, *Venezuela: Issues for Congress*, by Mark P. Sullivan.

[9] Joint Hearing on "Venezuela's Sanctionable Activities," House Committee on Foreign Affairs, Subcommittee on the Western Hemisphere and Subcommittee on the Middle East and South Asia, and House Committee on Oversight and Government Reform, Subcommittee on National Security, Homeland Defense and Foreign Operations. State Department testimony of Ambassador Daniel Benjamin, Coordinator for Counterterrorism; Kevin Whitaker, Acting Deputy Assistant Secretary for Western Hemisphere Affairs; and Thomas Delare, Director of the Terrorist Finance and Economic Sanctions Policy, Bureau of Economic, Energy, and Business Affairs, June 24, 2011, available at http://foreignaffairs.house.gov/112/ben062411.pdf

[10] Ibid.

Venezuela and FARC-Related Sanctions

To date, the United States has imposed financial sanctions against seven current or former Venezuelan government and military officials for providing support to the FARC. In September 2008, the Treasury Department froze the assets of two senior intelligence officials—General Hugo Carvajal and General Henry Rangel—and the former interior minister, Ramón Rodríguez Chacín, for allegedly helping the FARC with weapons and drug trafficking.[11] General Rangel was appointed by President Chávez as defense minister in January 2012, an action that raised concern among U.S. policymakers.

In September 2011, the Treasury Department imposed financial sanctions on four more Venezuelan officials for acting for or on behalf of the FARC, often in direct support of its narcotics and arms trafficking activities: Amilcar Jesus Figueroa Salazar, a member of Venezuela's delegation to the Latin American Parliament; Major General Cliver Antonio Alcala Cordones of the Venezuelan Army; Freddy Alirio Bernal Rosales, a national legislator for the United Socialist Party of Venezuela (PSUV); and Ramon Isidro Madriz Moreno, an officer of Venezuela's intelligence service.[12] In January 2012, President Chávez appointed General Henry Rangel as defense minister.

Iran's Activity and Influence in Latin America

Iran's Strategic Interest in Latin America[13]

The extent of Iran's relations with Latin American countries varies widely. While relations with Venezuela appear to be the most extensive, Iran's engagement in other countries appears to be much less than Iran trumpets for public consumption. No matter the scope of Iran's involvement in Latin America, Iran's key foreign policy focus remains its immediate region. It is in the Middle East and South and Central Asia where Iran perceives that threats to its survival may emanate, and in which Iran has, for ideological, religious, and political motives, tried to alter political outcomes in its favor. Whatever efforts Iran is making to engage like-minded leaders in Latin America, these efforts pale by comparison to its level of involvement in countries such as Iraq, Afghanistan, Syria, or Lebanon, in which Iran's Islamic Revolutionary Guard Corps—Qods Force personnel are on the ground consistently, funneling arms and funds to pro-Iranian movements and parties.[14] Interactions with national leaders and faction leaders in Middle Eastern and South and Central Asian countries such as these are frequent.

Since Mahmoud Ahmadinejad became Iran's President in August 2005, Iran has become progressively more isolated internationally, and subject to increasingly strict U.S., U.N., and multilateral sanctions. Sanctions imposed by the United States and the European Union in late 2011 and January 2012, to go into full effect by the summer of 2012, threaten Iran's vital

---

[11] Phil Gunson, op. cit., September 13, 2008; *Federal Register*, September 19, 2008, pp. 54453-54454.

[12] U.S. Department of the Treasury, "Treasury Designates Four Venezuelan Officials for Providing Arms and Security to the FARC," Press Center, September 8, 2011.

[13] This subsection was authored by Kenneth Katzman, CRS Specialist in Middle Eastern Affairs. For additional background on Iran, see: CRS Report RL32048, *Iran: U.S. Concerns and Policy Responses*, by Kenneth Katzman.

[14] U.S. Department of State, "Country Reports on Terrorism: 2010," Released August 18, 2011. available at: http://www.state.gov/j/ct/rls/crt/2010/170260 htm

lifeline—its exportation of crude oil.[15] Iran's progressive isolation at the hands of the United States and other "like minded countries" has caused Iran to cast about for new allies. In doing so, Iran naturally looks to other countries that are adversaries, or at least not allies, of the United States. Such states include some in Latin America, such as Venezuela and Cuba; several countries in Africa, such as Zimbabwe; North Korea; and Belarus. Iran has tried to persuade larger countries that have extensive but uneven relations with the United States, such as Russia and China, to brake U.S. efforts to further penalize Iran. Building relationships with these countries supports the assertions of Iran's leaders that U.S.-led efforts to isolate Iran are failing. The relationships also help Iran, at the margins, reduce the effects of sanctions, although the cumulative effects on Iran's economy are increasingly apparent and extensive.[16] Ties to Latin American countries not only serve these interests, but also potentially help Iran build leverage against the United States because of Latin America's geographic proximity to the United States. Director of National Intelligence James Clapper testified before the Senate Select Committee on Intelligence on January 31, 2012, that the recent plot to assassinate the Saudi Ambassador in Washington, DC, "shows that some Iranian officials—probably including Supreme Leader Ali Khamenei—have changed their calculus and are now more willing to conduct an attack in the United States in response to real or perceived U.S. actions that threaten the regime." Clapper further stated that "we are also concerned about Iranian plotting against U.S. or allied interests overseas."[17]

Iran's Growing Relations in Latin America

Over the past several years, there has been concern among policymakers about Iran's growing interest and activities in Latin America, particularly its relations with Venezuela under President Hugo Chávez, although there has been disagreement over the extent and significance of Iran's relations with the region. The January 2012 visit by Iranian President Mahmoud Ahmadinejad on a four-nation tour to Cuba, Ecuador, Nicaragua, and Venezuela increased concerns of some policymakers about Iran's efforts to deepen ties with Latin America.

Iran's ties to the region predate its recent increased attention. Venezuela's relations with Iran have been long-standing because they were both founding members of OPEC in 1960. In the aftermath of the 1979 Iranian revolution, Iran fostered closer relations with Cuba and with Nicaragua (after the 1979 Sandinista revolution). Under the government of President Mohammed Khatami (1997-2005), Iran made efforts to increase its trade with Latin America, particularly Brazil, and there were also efforts to increase cooperation with Venezuela. Venezuelan President Hugo Chávez visited Iran in 2001 and 2003, which led to a joint venture agreement to produce tractors in Venezuela.[18]

---

[15] For a detailed discussion of U.S., U.N., and multilateral sanctions against Iran, see CRS Report RS20871, *Iran Sanctions*, by Kenneth Katzman.

[16] Robert Worth, "Iran's Middle Class on Edge as World Presses In," *New York Times*, February 7, 2012.

[17] Testimony of Director of National Intelligence James Clapper before the Senate Select Committee on Intelligence, "Unclassified Statement for the Record on the Worldwide Threat Assessment of the U.S. Intelligence Community for the Senate Select Committee on Intelligence," January 31, 2012, available at: http://intelligence.senate.gov/120131/clapper.pdf

[18] Farideh Farhi "Tehran's Perspective on Iran-Latin American Relations," in *Iran in Latin America: Threat or 'Axis of Annoyance'?*, Woodrow Wilson International Center for Scholars, 2009 (based on July 2008 conference), edited by Cynthia Arnson, Haleh Esfandiari, and Adam Stubits, available at: http://www.wilsoncenter.org/sites/default/files/Iran_in_LA.pdf

Not until President Ahmadinejad's rule began in 2005, however, did Iran aggressively work to increase its diplomatic and economic linkages with Latin American countries. A major rationale for this increased focus on Latin America has been Iran's efforts to overcome its international isolation. The personal relationship between Ahmadinejad and Chávez also has driven the strengthening of bilateral ties. The two nations have signed a variety of agreements in agriculture, petrochemicals, oil exploration in the Orinoco region of Venezuela, the manufacturing of automobiles, and housing. During an April 2009 trip to Tehran, Chávez and Ahmadinejad inaugurated a new development bank for economic projects in both countries, with each country reportedly providing $100 million in initial capital. Weekly flights between the two countries began in 2007, but were curtailed in September 2010.[19] The State Department had expressed concern about these flights, maintaining that they were only subject to cursory immigration and customs controls.

Venezuela also has played a key role in the development of Iran's expanding relations with other countries in the region. This outreach has largely focused on leftist governments that share the goal of reducing U.S. influence in the region. In recent years, Iran's relations have grown with Bolivia under President Evo Morales, with Ecuador under President Rafael Correa, and with Nicaragua under President Daniel Ortega. While Iran has promised significant assistance and investment to these countries, observers maintain that there is little evidence that such promises have been fulfilled.[20] In Nicaragua for example, Iran has not followed through on its promise to finance the construction of a deep-water port. An Iranian project that has gone forward in Nicaragua is the construction of a hospital in 2009.[21] Likewise in Bolivia and Ecuador, there has been little evidence showing that Iran has followed up on its promises of investment. Nevertheless, in late August 2010, Iran announced that it would provide a $250 million loan to Bolivia for the construction of dairy, textile, cement, and other plants, and geological prospecting for minerals such as uranium and lithium.[22] According to January 31, 2012, congressional testimony by Director of National Intelligence James Clapper, "ties with Tehran offer some regional governments a means of staking an independent position on Iran—thereby mitigating its isolation—while also attempting to extract Iranian financial aid and investment for economic and social projects."[23]

Iran's trade with Latin America is miniscule, and for most countries in the region, non-existent. What trade there is largely consists of Latin American exports to Iran. In 2011, Brazil and Argentina were the largest traders in the region with Iran. Brazil exported some $2.3 billion in products to Iran in 2011, with beef and corn accounting for more than half, although Brazil's total

---

[19] "House Foreign Affairs, Subcommittee on Middle East and South Asia, and Subcommittee on Western Hemisphere, and House Oversight and Government Reform, Subcommittee on National Security, Homeland Defense and Foreign Operations Hold Joint Hearing on Venezuela's Sanctionable Activity," *CQ Congressional Transcripts*, June 24, 2011; and "House Foreign Affairs Committee Holds Hearing on Threats and Security in the Western Hemisphere," *CQ Congressional Transcripts*, October 13, 2011.

[20] For example, see Kavon "Hak" Hakimzadeh, "Iran & Venezuela: The Axis of Annoyance," *Military Review*, May 1, 2009; and Anne-Marie O'Connor and Mary Beth Sheridan, "Iran's Invisible Nicaragua Embassy; Feared Stronghold Never Materialized," *Washington Post*, July 13, 2009. Also see "House Foreign Affairs Committee Holds Hearing on Democracy in Nicaragua," *CQ Congressional Transcripts*, December 1, 2011.

[21] Steve Stecklow and Farnaz Fassihi, "Iran's Global Foray Has Mixed Results," *Wall Street Journal*, September 28, 2009.

[22] "Iran Announces 250m Dollar-Loan to Bolivia to Assist Uranium Prospecting," *BBC Monitoring Americas*, September 1, 2010.

[23] Testimony of Director of National Intelligence James Clapper, January 31, 2012, op. cit.

---

exports to Iran represented less than 1% of Brazil's exports globally. Argentina's exports to Iran amounted to almost $1 billion in 2011 (largely vegetable oils, animal feed, and corn), but accounted for just 1.6% of Argentina's total exports.[24]

On the diplomatic front, Iran has opened embassies over the past several years in Bolivia, Ecuador, and Nicaragua, as well as in Chile, Colombia, and Uruguay. This is in addition to existing embassies in Argentina, Brazil, Cuba, Mexico, and Venezuela.[25] Iran has also reportedly opened 17 cultural centers in the region in recent years.[26] In late January 2012, Iran also launched a Spanish-language satellite TV network as part of its ideological battle to counter what it views as biased reporting—President Ahmadinejad said that it would help end the West's "hegemony" of the airwaves.[27] Reports that Iran was building a large embassy in Managua, Nicaragua (which even Secretary of State Hillary Clinton noted in public remarks) turned out to be erroneous.[28] Other reports that Iran's embassy in Venezuela is one of the largest in the world were also inaccurate. State Department officials maintain that there are many embassies in Caracas that have a diplomatic presence far larger than that of Iran, including the U.S. Embassy.[29]

Ahmadinejad's January 2012 Trip to Latin America

Since 2006, President Ahmadinejad has visited Venezuela several times, and has also visited Bolivia, Brazil, Ecuador, Nicaragua, and Cuba. In early May 2009, a scheduled first trip by Ahmadinejad to Brazil was unexpectedly postponed until after Iran's election in June. There had been some protests in Brazil against Ahmadinejad's visit, but the trip ultimately took place in November 2009. Brazilian President Lula da Silva maintained that the West should not isolate Iran. On the same trip, the Iranian president once again visited Bolivia and Venezuela.[30]

Iranian President Ahmadinejad began his fifth official visit to the region on January 8, 2012, stopping in Venezuela to meet with President Chávez. This was followed by attendance at the presidential inauguration of Daniel Ortega in Nicaragua on January 10, and then visits to Cuba and Ecuador. As in the past, the main purpose of the trip was to shore up relations with these countries as a means of overcoming Iran's international isolation. All four countries expressed support for Iran's peaceful development of nuclear power. The trip occurred at a time when Ahmadinejad is facing significant problems at home, including a difficult economic situation exacerbated by international economic sanctions related to Iran's nuclear ambitions, and a political conflict in Iran between Ahmadinejad and other conservatives, including Iran's supreme leader.[31]

---

[24] Statistics drawn from *Global Trade Atlas*, which utilizes trade statistics reported by countries worldwide.

[25] Anne-Marie O'Connor and Mary Beth Sheridan, "Iran's Invisible Nicaragua Embassy; Feared Stronghold Never Materialized," *Washington Post*, July 13, 2009.

[26] "Sen. Carl Levin Holds a Hearing on the F.Y. 1012 Authorization for the U.S. Northern Command and the U.S. Southern Command—Committee Hearing," *Political Transcripts by CQ Transcriptions*, April 5, 2011.

[27] Jim Wyss, "Iran's HispanTV Aims to Woo Latino Viewers," *Miami Herald*, January 31, 2012.

[28] Ibid; and Sylvie Lanteaume, "Iran's Hand in Latin America Not as U.S. Feared," *Agence France Presse*, July 14, 2009.

[29] "House Foreign Affairs, Subcommittee on Middle East and South Asia, and Subcommittee on Western Hemisphere, and House Oversight and Government Reform, Subcommittee on National Security, Homeland Defense and Foreign Operations Hold Joint Hearing on Venezuela's Sanctionable Activity," *CQ Congressional Transcripts*, June 24, 2011

[30] Juan Forero, "Ahmadinejad Boosts Latin American Ties," *Washington Post*, November 28, 2009.

[31] For background on Iran's current political and economic situation, see: CRS Report RL32048, *Iran: U.S. Concerns* (continued...)

Although President Ahmadinejad signed a number of agreements during his tour, it is doubtful that this will lead to significant Iranian investment or financial support. Analysts point out that leaders' statements during these trips are largely propaganda, with the official Iranian press trumpeting relations with these countries in order to show that Iran is not isolated internationally and that it has good relations with countries geographically close to the United States.[32] The trip was restricted to meeting with four leftist governments that have often opposed U.S. policy in the region and have limited regional influence. The fact that the tour notably did not include a trip to Brazil to meet with President Dilma Rousseff detracted from the significance of the visit to the region. A close adviser to Ahmadinejad maintained in an interview in the Brazilian press that President Rousseff had "destroyed years of good relations" between Iran and Brazil.[33] Some press accounts characterized Ahmadinejad's tour of the region as "lackluster" and a mere diplomatic show attempting to remind the world that Iran continues to have relations with countries in Latin America.[34] Director of National Intelligence James Clapper testified before Congress in late January 2012 that while the U.S. intelligence community remains concerned about Iran's connection with Venezuela, Ahmadinejad's recent trip to Latin America "was not all that successful."[35]

On the first stop of the trip, Iran and Venezuela signed cooperation agreements in industry, science and technology, and politics. The agreements reportedly included training, studies, workshops and professional exchanges in nanotechnology; the creation of bi-national groups on development needs and complementary productive activities; and technology transfer in areas of agriculture, food industry, mining, and construction. Venezuela and Iran reportedly have signed more than 270 accords over the past decade, including agreements on construction projects (including housing, agricultural and food plants, and corn processing plants), car and tractor factories, energy initiatives, and banking programs.[36] During the Iranian president's recent trip, President Chávez maintained that Venezuela was showing its solidarity with Iran since it is "one of the targets that Yankee imperialism has in its sights."[37]

During Ahmadinejad's visit to Nicaragua, President Daniel Ortega defended Iran's peaceful nuclear program while the Iranian president, comparing the Iranian and Nicaragua revolutions, maintained that both countries were "fighting to establish solidarity and justice."[38] Ortega's friendship with Ahmadinejad and Chávez reportedly has many Nicaraguans questioning their president's foreign policy, with some expressing concerns that such relationships could jeopardize

---

(...continued)

and Policy Responses, by Kenneth Katzman.

[32] Comments by Stephen Johnson, Center for Strategic and International Studies, and Afshin Molavi, New America Foundation, at a January 19, 2012, event sponsored by the Council of the Americas (Washington, D.C.) on "Iran in the Americas: A Readout of the Visit."

[33] Simon Romero, "Iranian Adviser Accuses Brazil of Ruining Relations," *New York Times*, January 24, 2012. Subsequently, the Iranian adviser denied part of the interview, and stressed that relations between Iran and Brazil are good, see "Iranian Aide Says Foreign Media Distorted His Interview on Ties with Brazil," *BBC Monitoring Newsfile* (text of report by Iranian official government news agency IRNA) January 24, 2012.

[34] Brian Ellsworth, "Iranian Leader Ends Lackluster Latin America Tour," *Reuters News*, January 13, 2012.

[35] "Senate Select Intelligence Committee Holds Hearing on Worldwide Threats," *CQ Congressional Transcripts*, January 31, 2012.

[36] "Ahmadinejad, Chávez Reiterate Efforts to Enhance World Peace," *FARS News Agency*, January 13, 2012.

[37] "Chávez and Ahmadinejad Taunt U.S. Over "Big Atomic Bomb," *The Times* (London), January 10, 2012.

[38] "Nicaragua's President Urges Denuclearization of Israel," *FARS News Agency*, January 11, 2012; "Ahmadinejad Underlines Identical Traits of Iranian, Nicaraguan Revolutions," *FARS News Agency*, January 11, 2012.

Nicaragua's relations with the United States and other Western countries. In the case of Iran, some question what Nicaragua is getting out of the relationship.[39] Nicaraguan officials were reportedly upset that during Ahmadinejad's visit, Iran did not provide debt relief for the $164 million borrowed in the 1980s for shipments of petroleum.[40]

In Cuba, Ahmadinejad met with President Raúl Castro as well as former leader Fidel Castro. While addressing an audience at the University of Havana (where he received an honorary doctorate of political science) Ahmadinejad denounced capitalism, maintaining that it was "a failed system in decay."[41] A joint statement by Raúl Castro and the Iranian president highlighted the "right of all nations to the peaceful use of nuclear energy."[42]

In Ecuador, the last leg of Ahmadinejad's Latin America tour, the Iranian president and President Rafael Correa held talks on trade, agriculture, technology, and cooperation in oil and energy. Ahmadinejad also reportedly suggested the establishment of a direct flight between Tehran and Quito as a means of fortifying commercial engagement.[43] President Correa also reiterated his support for Iran's peaceful nuclear program and criticized both the United States and the International Atomic Energy Agency.[44]

Concerns about Iran's Military and Potential Terrorist Activities

An April 2010 unclassified Department of Defense report to Congress on Iran's military power (required by Section 1245 of the National Defense Authorization Act for FY2010, P.L. 111-84) maintained that Iran's Qods Force, which maintains operational capabilities around the world, has increased its presence in Latin America in recent years, particularly in Venezuela.[45] Despite the report, the commander of the U.S. Southern Command, General Douglas Fraser, maintains that the focus of Iran in the region has been diplomatic and commercial, and that he has not seen an increase in Iran's military presence in the region.[46]

In October 2011, the Department of Justice filed criminal charges against a dual Iranian-American citizen from Texas, Manssor Arbabsiar, and a member of Iran's Qods Force in Iran, Gholam Shakuri, for their alleged participation in a bizarre plot to kill the Saudi Ambassador in Washington, DC. The indictment alleges that Arbabsiar met several times in Mexico City with an

---

[39] Dave Graham, "Nicaraguans Worry About Ortega's Foreign Friends," *Reuters News*, January 17, 2012.

[40] "Nicaraguan Government Upset Iranian President Failed To Write Off Debt—Paper," *BBC Monitoring Americas*, January 14, 2012 (text of report from *El Nuevo Diario* [Nicaragua], January 11, 2012).

[41] Francisco Jara, "In Cuba, Iran Leader Says Capitalism 'In Decay,'" *Agence France Presse*, January 11, 2012.

[42] "Iran, Cuba Agree on 'Peaceful Use of Nuclear Energy,'" *Platts Commodity News*, January 12, 2012.

[43] "Ahmadinejad Plantea Vuelos Entre Teherán y Quito Para Fortalecer Comercio," *Agence France Presse*, January 16, 2012.

[44] "Correa Reitera Apoyo a Program Nuclear Iraní y Critica a Estados Unidos," *Agence France Presse*, January 14, 2012.

[45] Department of Defense, "Unclassified Report on Military Power of Iran," April 2010. For the full text of the report, see http://www.politico.com/static/PPM145_link_042010.html. For background on the Qods Force, see CRS Report RL32048, *Iran: U.S. Concerns and Policy Responses*, by Kenneth Katzman.

[46] *Anne Flaherty, "Pentagon Says Iran's Reach in Latin America Doesn't Pose Military Threat,"* AP Newswire, April 27, 2010. General Fraser reiterated that Iran's focus in Latin America has been "primarily diplomatic and commercial," in March 30, 2011, testimony before the House Armed Services Committee. See: "Hearing of the House Armed Services Committee; Subject FY2012 National Defense Authorization Budget Requests for the U.S. Southern Command, U.S. Northern Command, and U.S. European Command," *Federal News Service*, March 30, 2011.

---

informant of the U.S. Drug Enforcement Administration (DEA) posing as a member of Mexico's most violent drug trafficking organization, Los Zetas, and had arranged to hire the informant to murder the Ambassador with the financial support of Shakuri.[47] Other alleged plans reportedly included plots to pay Los Zetas to bomb the Israeli Embassy in Washington, DC, and the Saudi and Israeli Embassies in Buenos Aires.[48] Some Iran experts have expressed skepticism about the alleged plots, maintaining that the details do not reflect a pattern used by the Qods Force in foreign operations.[49] The DEA testified in November 2011 that the alleged plot "illustrates the extent to which terrorist organizations will align themselves with other criminals to achieve their goals."[50] As noted above, Director of National Intelligence James Clapper stated before the Senate Select Committee on Intelligence in late January 2012 that the recent plot to kill the Saudi Ambassador shows that "some Iranian officials … are now more willing to conduct an attack in the United States," and he expressed concern "about Iranian plotting against U.S. or allied interests overseas."[51]

In December 2011, a documentary featured on the Spanish-language network *Univisión* alleged that Iranian and Venezuelan diplomats in Mexico tried to recruit Mexican students for plotting possible cyberattacks against the United States. There is no indication that U.S. officials have been able to corroborate the allegations in the documentary. Subsequently, a Venezuelan diplomat based in Mexico at the time, Livia Acosta, who was recorded participating in the discussion with the Mexican students, was declared persona non grata by the State Department on January 8, 2012, and asked to leave the United States from her position as Venezuelan Consul General in Miami.

Venezuela and Iran-Related Sanctions

Another rationale for Ahmadinejad's increased focus on Latin America, closely related to the goal of overcoming Iran's international isolation, has been to circumvent U.S. and U.N. sanctions on Iran.

To date, the United States has imposed sanctions on two companies in Venezuela because of connections to Iran's proliferation activities. In August 2008, the State Department imposed sanctions on the Venezuelan Military Industries Company (CAVIM) pursuant to the Iran, North Korea, and Syria Nonproliferation Act (P.L. 109-353) for allegedly violating a ban on technology that could assist Iran in the development of weapons systems.[52] The sanctions prohibited any U.S.

---

[47] U.S. Department of Justice, "Two Men Charged in Alleged Plot to Assassinate Saudi Arabian Ambassador to the United States," Press Release, October 11, 2011, available at http://www.justice.gov/opa/pr/2011/October/11-ag-1339.html.

[48] Charles Savage and Scott Shane, "Iranians Accused of a Plot to Kill Saudis' U.S. Envoy," *New York Times*, October 12, 2011; and Siobhan Gorman, Devlin Barrett, and Stephanie Simon, "U.S. News: Accusations Against Iran Fleshed Out," *Wall Street Journal*, October 13, 2011.

[49] Farnaz Fassihi, "U.S. News: Iran Experts Question Qods Role in Alleged Terror Plot," *Wall Street Journal*, October 13, 2011. Also see CRS Report RL32048, *Iran: U.S. Concerns and Policy Responses*, by Kenneth Katzman.

[50] U.S. Congress, House Committee on Foreign Affairs, Subcommittee on Terrorism, Nonproliferation, and Trade, *Narcoterrorism and the Long Reach of U.S. Law Enforcement, Part II*, 112th Cong., 1st sess., November 17, 2011, Serial No. 112-81 (Washington: GPO, 2011), written testimony of Derek S. Maltz, Special Agent in charge of the Special Operations Division, Drug Enforcement Administration, available at: http://foreignaffairs.house.gov/112/mal111711.pdf

[51] Testimony of Director of National Intelligence James Clapper, January 31, 2012, op. cit.

[52] Although the sanction became effective in August 2008, it was not published in the *Federal Register* until October (continued...)

---

government procurement or assistance to the company. While these sanctions expired in 2010, they were imposed once again on May 23, 2011, for a two-year period.[53] In October 2008, the U.S. Treasury Department imposed sanctions on an Iranian-owned bank based in Caracas, the Banco Internacional de Desarollo, C.A., under Executive Order 13382 that allows the President to block the assets of proliferators of weapons of mass destruction and their supporters. The bank is linked to the Export Development Bank of Iran (EDBI), which the Treasury Department asserts has provided or attempted to provide services to Iran's Ministry of Defense and Armed Forces Logistics.[54]

In May 2011, the United States imposed sanctions on Venezuela's state oil company, Petróleos de Venezuela S.A. (PdVSA), pursuant to the Comprehensive Iran Sanctions, Accountability, and Disinvestment Act of 2010 (P.L. 111-195) because the company provided $50 million worth of reformate, an additive used in gasoline, to Iran between December 2010 and March 2011. Specifically, the State Department imposed three sanctions on PdVSA to prohibit it from competing for U.S. government procurement contracts, securing financing from the Export-Import Bank, and obtaining U.S. export licenses. The sanctions specifically exclude PdVSA subsidiaries (Citgo) and do not prohibit the export of oil to the United States.[55]

Past Venezuelan comments about potential Iranian support for the development of nuclear energy in Venezuela raised concerns among U.S. officials and other observers. In September 2009, President Chávez announced during a visit to Iran that Venezuela was working on a preliminary plan for the construction of a "nuclear village" in Venezuela with Iranian assistance so that "the Venezuelan people can count in the future on this marvelous resource for peaceful purposes."[56] The transfer of Iranian nuclear technology from Iran would be a violation of U.N. Security Council Resolutions—1737 (2006), 1747 (2007), and 1803 (2008)—that imposed restrictions on Iran's nuclear technology transfers. In September 2010, President Chávez maintained that his government was carrying out initial studies into starting a nuclear energy program. In October 2010, Russia agreed to help Venezuela build its first nuclear power plant, but in March 2011, in the aftermath of Japan's nuclear plant disaster, President Chávez said that he was freezing plans for a nuclear power program.[57]

In September 2009, comments by Venezuelan officials offered conflicting information about Iran's support for Venezuela's search for uranium deposits. Venezuelan Minister of Basic Industry and Mining Rodolfo Sanz said that Iran was assisting Venezuela in detecting uranium reserves in the west and southwest of Venezuela.[58] Subsequently, however, Venezuela's Minister of Science,

---

(...continued)

2008. See *Federal Register*, pp. 63226-63227, October 23, 2008.

[53] U.S. Department of State, "Iran, North Korea and Syria Nonproliferation Act (INKSNA)," Fact Sheet, May 24, 2011.

[54] U.S. Department of the Treasury, Press Release, "Export Development Bank of Iran Designated as a Proliferator," October 22, 2008.

[55] U.S. Department of State, "Seven Companies Sanctioned Under the Amended Iran Sanctions Act," Fact Sheet, May 24, 2011.

[56] "Iran Will Not Back Down on Nuclear Energy: Hugo Chávez" *Agence France Presse*, September 4, 2009.

[57] "Hugo Chávez Says Venezuela Is Studying Idea of Starting Peaceful Nuclear Energy Program," *AP Newswire*, September 28, 2010; "Russia to Build Nuclear Power Plant in Venezuela," *Reuters News*, October 15, 2010; Diego Ore, "Venezuela Halts Nuclear Program After Japan Disaster," *Reuters News*, March 15, 2011.

[58] See the following press reports: "Iran Helps Venezuela Find Uranium Deposits," *BBC Monitoring Caucasus*, September 26, 2009; and "Iran Helps Venezuela Find Uranium Deposits," *Tehran Press TV Online*, September 26, 2009.

Technology, and Intermediary Industry Jesse Chacon denied that Iran was helping Venezuela seek uranium, while Venezuela's Minister of Energy Rafael Ramirez maintained that Venezuela has yet to develop a plan to explore or exploit its uranium deposits.[59] Observers point out that Venezuela does not yet mine uranium. U.N. Security Council Resolution 1929 (June 9, 2010) bars Iranian investment in uranium mining projects abroad.

In November 2010 and again in May 2011, an online German publication, *Die Welt*, alleged that Venezuela and Iran had signed an agreement in October 2010 for a jointly operated missile base in Venezuela.[60] The Department of State, however, maintains that there is no evidence to support such claims, and that that there is no reason to believe that the assertions are credible.[61] Venezuela's foreign minister called the reports by the German newspaper "an extravagant lie."[62]

Concerns about Hezbollah in Latin America

Another reason for U.S. concerns about Iran's deepening relations with Latin America is its ties to the radical Lebanon-based Islamic Shiite group Hezbollah, a State Department-designated Foreign Terrorist Organization. Hezbollah, along with Iran, is reported to have been linked to two bombings against Jewish targets in Argentina in the early 1990s: the 1992 bombing of the Israeli Embassy in Buenos Aires that killed 30 people and the 1994 bombing of the Argentine-Israeli Mutual Association (AMIA) in Buenos Aires that killed 85 people.

In recent years, U.S. concerns regarding Hezbollah in Latin America have focused on its fundraising activities among sympathizers in the region, particularly the tri-border area (TBA) of Argentina, Brazil, and Paraguay (see **Figure 2**).[63] (At the same time, U.S. officials point out that Hezbollah's primary funding is from Iran, and not from fundraising activities in Latin America.) The Brazilian city of Foz do Iguaçu and the Paraguayan city of Ciudad del Este have large Muslim populations. The TBA has long been used for arms and drug trafficking, contraband smuggling, document and currency fraud, money laundering, and the manufacture and movement of pirated goods. A 2009 RAND study examined how Hezbollah has benefitted from film piracy proceeds in the TBA.[64]

For several years, the State Department's annual report on terrorism reiterated U.S. concerns regarding fundraising activities by sympathizers of Hezbollah (and the Sunni Muslim Palestinian group Hamas) in the TBA, but the report also consistently asserted that "that there was no corroborated information ... that these or other Islamic extremist groups had an operational presence in the region."[65] The State Department's 2010 terrorism report (issued in August 2011)

---

[59] "Venezuela Denies Iran is Helping It," *New York Times*, September 27, 2009; and Fabian Cambero, "Interview: Venezuela Says No Plans Yet on Exploring Uranium," *Reuters*, September 27, 2009.

[60] "Iran Planning to Build Missile Base in Venezuela," November 25, 2010, and "Venezuela, Iran Press Ahead with Missile Base," May 13, 2011, website of *Die Welt* online (as translated by Open Source Center).

[61] CRS correspondence with Department of State, January 5, 2011, and May 23, 2011; "Chávez Mocks Missile Base Reports," *CNN Wire*, June 1, 2011.

[62] "Chávez Mocks Missile Base Reports," *CNN Wire*, June 1, 2011.

[63] For additional background, see *Threat Convergence in South America's Tri-Border Area (TBA)*, The Fund for Peace, Center for the Study of Threat Convergence, Factsheet Series, January 11, 2010; and Rensselaer Lee, "Dispatches: The Tri-Border-Terrorism Nexus," *Global Crime*, Vol. 9, No 4, November 2008.

[64] Gregory F. Treverton et al., *Film Piracy, Organized Crime, and Terrorism*, RAND, 2009.

[65] U.S. Department of State, "Country Reports on Terrorism 2009," August 5, 2010.

---

asserted more broadly that there were no known operational cells of either Al Qaeda or Hezbollah-related groups in the hemisphere, but noted that "ideological sympathizers in South America and the Caribbean continued to provide financial and moral support to these and other terrorist groups in the Middle East and South Asia."[66] In March 2011 congressional testimony, General Douglas Fraser, commander of the U.S. Southern Command, maintained that he had not seen Hezbollah or Hamas growing in any capacity in the region, and reiterated that "primarily any support that they are giving is financial support, principally back to parent organizations in the Middle East."[67]

Figure 2. Tri-Border Area of Argentina, Brazil, and Paraguay

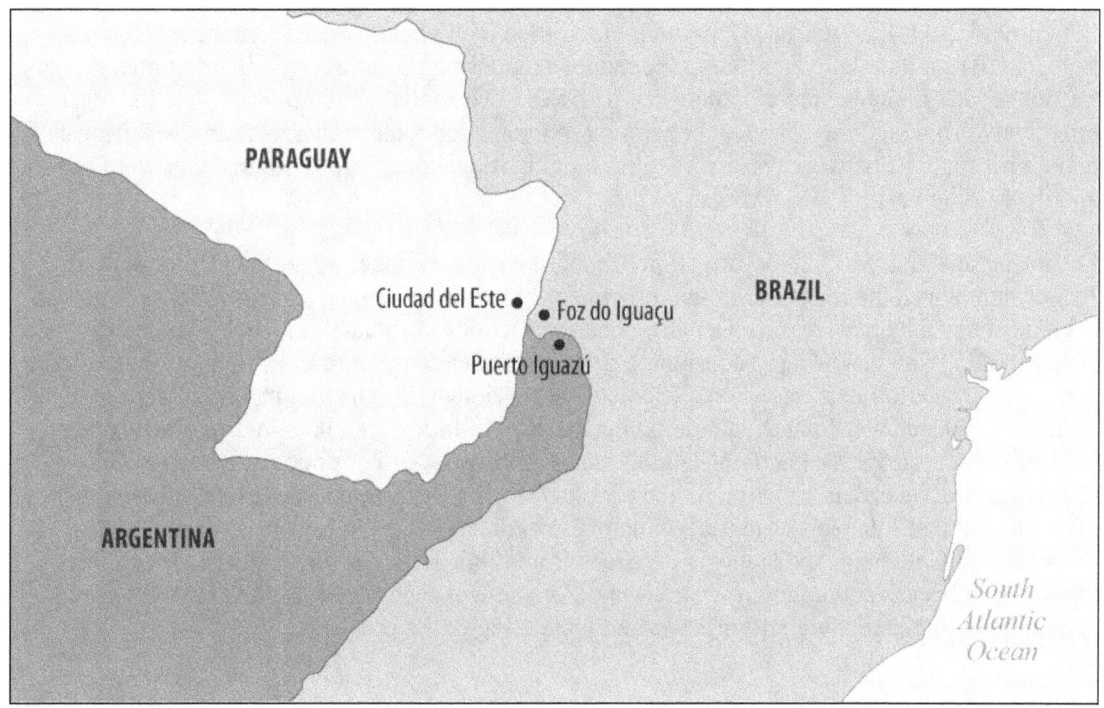

Source: CRS.

Hezbollah-Related Sanctions

The United States has imposed sanctions on individuals and companies in the region for providing support to Hezbollah. Since 2006, the Treasury Department has sanctioned over a dozen individuals and several entities in the TBA for providing financial support to Hezbollah leadership in Lebanon.[68] In December 2010, the Treasury Department sanctioned Hezbollah's

---

[66] U.S. Department of State, "Country Reports on Terrorism 2010," August 18, 2011, available at http://www.state.gov/s/ct/rls/crt/2010/index htm

[67] House Armed Services Committee Holds Hearing on the Defense Authorization Proposed Budget Requests for Fiscal 2012 and Future Years on the U.S. Southern Command, U.S. Northern Command, and U.S. European Command," *CQ Congressional Transcripts*, March 30, 2011.

[68] U.S. Congress, House Committee on Foreign Affairs, *Emerging Threats and Security in the Western Hemisphere: Next Steps for U.S. Policy*, 112th Cong., 1st sess., October 13, 2011, Serial No. 112-75 (Washington: GPO, 2011), written testimony of U.S. Department of the Treasury's Assistant Secretary for Terrorist Financing Daniel L. Glaser available at: http://foreignaffairs.house.gov/112/gla101311.pdf

chief representative in South America, Bilal Mohsen Wehbe, for transferring funds collected in Brazil to Lebanon. He also reportedly has been responsible for overseeing Hezbollah's counterintelligence activities in the TBA.[69]

Beyond the TBA, U.S. officials have expressed concern that Hezbollah is able to tap into the large Lebanese diaspora in Venezuela and elsewhere in Latin America.[70] In June 2008, the Treasury Department imposed sanctions on two Venezuelans—Ghazi Nasr al Din (a Venezuelan diplomat serving in Lebanon) and Fawzi Kan'an—for providing financial and other support to Hezbollah. U.S. citizens are prohibited from engaging in any transactions with the two Venezuelans, including any business with two travel agencies in Caracas owned by Kan'an.[71]

In February 2011, the Treasury Department identified the Lebanon-based Lebanese Canadian Bank (LCB) for its role in facilitating the money laundering activities of an international narcotics trafficking and money laundering network with ties to Hezbollah, and imposed sanctions that effectively prohibited the bank from operating in the United States. The Treasury Department maintained that the network was involved in moving illegal drugs from South America to Europe and the Middle East via West Africa.[72]

Following on from the U.S. investigation of the LCB, in November 2011, the Department of Justice announced the federal criminal indictment of Lebanese citizen Ayman Joumaa (who had been designated by the Treasury Department as a narcotics trafficker and money launder in January 2011) for conspiring to coordinate shipments of cocaine from Colombia through Central America for sale to Los Zetas, one of Mexico's most violent drug trafficking organizations. The indictment alleged that Joumaa laundered hundreds of millions of dollars in drug trafficking proceeds from Europe, Mexico, the United States, and West Africa for cocaine suppliers in Colombia and Venezuela.[73] A civil indictment filed by the Department of Justice in December 2011 alleged that Joumaa's drug trafficking organization operates in Lebanon, West Africa, Panama, and Colombia, and launders proceeds from illicit activities through various channels, including bulk cash smuggling operations and Lebanese exchange houses, and pays fees to Hezbollah to facilitate the transportation and laundering of the proceeds.[74]

U.S. Policy

As in other parts of the world, the United States has assisted Latin American and Caribbean nations over the years in their struggle against terrorist or insurgent groups indigenous to the

---

[69] "Treasury Targets Hizballah Financial Network," *Department of the Treasury Documents*, Press Release, December 9, 2010.

[70] House Committee on Foreign Affairs, *Emerging Threats and Security in the Western Hemisphere: Next Steps for U.S. Policy*, op. cit., written testimony of Philip S. Goldberg, Assistant Secretary, Bureau of Intelligence and Research, Department of State, available at: http://foreignaffairs house.gov/112/gol101311.pdf

[71] "Treasury Targets Hizballah in Venezuela," *States News Service*, June 18, 2008.

[72] U.S. Department of the Treasury, "Treasury Identifies Lebanese Canadian Bank Sal as a Primary Money Laundering Concern," Press Release, February 10, 2011.

[73] U.S. Department of Justice, U.S. Attorney's Office—Eastern District of Virginia, "U.S. Charges Alleged Lebanese Drug Kingpin with Laundering Drug Proceeds for Mexican and Colombian Drug Cartels," Press Release, December 13, 2011; Jo Becker, "Beirut Bank Seen as a Hub of Hezbollah's Financing," *New York Times*, December 14, 2011.

[74] U.S. Drug Enforcement Administration, "DEA News: Civil Suit Exposes Lebanese Money Laundering Scheme for Hizballah," News Release, December 15, 2011, available at: http://www.justice.gov/dea/pubs/pressrel/pr121511 html

---

region. For example, in the 1980s, the United States supported the government of El Salvador with significant economic and military assistance in its struggle against a leftist guerrilla insurgency. In recent years, the United States has employed various policy tools to combat terrorism in the Latin America and Caribbean region, including sanctions, anti-terrorism assistance and training, law enforcement cooperation, and multilateral cooperation through the OAS. Moreover, given the nexus between terrorism and drug trafficking, one can argue that assistance aimed at combating drug trafficking organizations in the Andean region has also been a means of combating terrorism by cutting off a source of revenue for terrorist organizations. The same argument can be made regarding efforts to combat money laundering in the region.

Although terrorism was not the main focus of U.S. policy toward the region in recent years, attention increased in the aftermath of the 9/11 terrorist attacks on New York and Washington. Anti-terrorism assistance has increased along with bilateral and regional cooperation against terrorism. Congress approved the Bush Administration's request in 2002 to expand the scope of U.S. assistance to Colombia beyond a counternarcotics focus to also include counterterrorism assistance to the government in its military efforts against drug-financed leftist guerrillas and rightist paramilitaries. Border security with Mexico also became a prominent issue in bilateral relations, with attention focused on the potential transit of terrorists through Mexico to the United States.

U.S. Sanctions

The United States has imposed sanctions on three groups in Colombia (ELN, FARC, and AUC) and one group in Peru (SL) designated by the Department of State as FTOs. Official designation of such groups as FTOs triggers a number of sanctions, including visa restrictions and the blocking of any funds of these groups in U.S. financial institutions. The designation also has the effect of increasing public awareness about these terrorist organizations and the concerns that the United States has about them. As noted above, the United States has included Cuba on its list of state sponsors of terrorism since 1982, pursuant to Section 6(j) of the EAA, and both Cuba and Venezuela are currently on the annual Section 40A AECA list of countries that are not cooperating fully with U.S. antiterrorism efforts, lists that trigger a number of sanctions.

As described above, the United States has also imposed financial sanctions on several Venezuelan government and military officials for supporting the FARC's weapons and drug trafficking, and has imposed sanctions on three Venezuelan companies for their support of Iran. With regard to Hezbollah, the United States has imposed sanctions on individuals and companies in the region—including in Venezuela and in the TBA of South America—for providing financial support to the organization. The Department of Justice is also pursing cases against entities and individuals involving a drug money laundering network in the region with ties to Hezbollah.

U.S. Assistance and Other Support

The United States provides assistance to improve Latin American countries' counterterrorism capabilities through several types of programs administered by the Department of State, including: an Anti-Terrorism Assistance (ATA) program, an Export Control and Related Border Security (EXBS) program, a Counterterrorism Financing (CTF) program, and a Terrorist Interdiction Program (TIP). All the programs are funded through the Nonproliferation, Anti-terrorism, Demining, and Related Programs (NADR) foreign aid funding account.

The largest of these is the ATA program, which over the years has provided training and equipment to Latin American countries to help improve their capabilities in such areas as airport security management, hostage negotiations, bomb detection and deactivation, and countering terrorism financing. Such training was expanded to Argentina in the aftermath of the two bombings in 1992 and 1994. Assistance was also stepped up in 1997 to Argentina, Brazil, and Paraguay in light of increased U.S. concern over illicit activities in the tri-border area of those countries. In recent years, ATA for Western Hemisphere countries amounted to $9.1 million in FY2008, $9.3 million in FY2009, an estimated $9.3 million in FY2010, and an estimated $12.75 million in FY2011. For FY2012, the Administration requested $12.28 million, with $2.25 million for Colombia, $4.18 million for Mexico and $5.85 million for other Latin American countries through a regional program.

The EXBS program helps countries develop export and border control systems in order to prevent states and terrorist organizations from acquiring weapons of mass destruction, their delivery systems, and destabilizing conventional weapons. Latin American countries received $7.1 million in EXBS assistance in FY2008, $2.1 million in FY2009, an estimated $2.925 million in FY2010, and an estimated $7.950 million in FY2011. The FY2012 request was for $3.25 million, with assistance slated for Argentina, Brazil, Chile, Mexico, Panama, and a regional program.

CTF assistance provides support in detecting, isolating, and dismantling terrorist financial networks. No CTF assistance was provided for Latin America in FY2008, while $225,000 was provided in FY2009, largely to Mexico, and an estimated $460,000 is being provided in FY2010 for countries under a regional program. No assistance was requested for the region for FY2011 or FY2012.

TIP assistance helps foreign immigration authorities with a computer database system that enables identification of suspected terrorists attempting to transit air, land, or sea ports of entry. No assistance was provided to the region in FY2008 or FY2009, but an estimated $1.3 million was provided for a Western Hemisphere regional program in FY2010 and an estimated $1 million in FY2011. The FY2012 request was for $1 million for a regional funding program.

A number of Latin American countries participate in U.S.-government port security programs administered by the Department of Homeland Security (DHS) and the Department of Energy. The Container Security Initiative (CSI) operated by the U.S. Customs and Border Protection of DHS uses a security regime to ensure that all containers that pose a potential risk for terrorism are identified and inspected at foreign ports before they are placed on vessels destined for the United States. Ten Latin American ports in Argentina, the Bahamas, Brazil, Colombia, the Dominican Republic, Honduras, Jamaica, and Panama participate in the CSI program. The Department of Energy's National Nuclear Security Administration administers the Megaports Initiative, a program which involves deploying radiation detection equipment in order to deter, detect, and interdict illicit trafficking in nuclear and radioactive materials. To date, the Megaports Initiative is operational in ports in the Bahamas, Colombia, the Dominican Republic, Honduras, Mexico, and Panama.

The Department of Homeland Security's Immigration and Customs Enforcement (ICE) has partnered with several Latin American countries to establish Trade Transparency Units that facilitate exchanges of information in order to combat trade-based money laundering. TTUs have been established in Argentina, Brazil, Colombia, Paraguay, and Mexico.

The United States also has worked closely with the governments of the tri-border area—Argentina, Brazil, and Paraguay—through the "3+1 regional cooperation mechanism," established in 2002 to serve as a forum for counterterrorism cooperation and prevention among all four countries.

Increased Regional Cooperation Since 9/11

Latin American nations strongly condemned the September 2001 terrorist attacks on the United States and took action through the OAS and the Rio Treaty to strengthen hemispheric cooperation against terrorism. The OAS, which happened to be meeting in Peru at the time, swiftly condemned the attacks, reiterated the need to strengthen hemispheric cooperation to combat terrorism, and expressed full solidarity with the United States. At a special session on September 19, 2001, OAS members invoked the 1947 Inter-American Treaty of Reciprocal Assistance, also known as the Rio Treaty, which obligates signatories to the treaty to come to one another's defense in case of outside attack. Another resolution approved on September 21, 2001, called on Rio Treaty signatories to "use all legally available measures to pursue, capture, extradite, and punish those individuals" involved in the attacks and to "render additional assistance and support to the United States, as appropriate, to address the September 11 attacks, and also to prevent future terrorist acts."

In the aftermath of 9/11, OAS members reinvigorated efforts of the of the Inter-American Committee on Terrorism (CICTE) to combat terrorism in the hemisphere. The CICTE has cooperated on border security mechanisms, controls to prevent terrorist funding, and law enforcement and counterterrorism intelligence and information.[75] It was worked on a wide range of capacity building and training programs including border controls (covering maritime and aviation security, customs, and immigration), critical infrastructure protection (covering cybersecurity, major events security, and tourism security), counter-terrorism legislative assistance and combating terrorism financing, and strengthening strategies on emerging terrorist threats. At the CICTE's 11th regular session held in March 2011, member states issued a declaration of renewed hemispheric commitment to enhance cooperation to prevent, combat, and eliminate terrorism.[76]

OAS members signed the Inter-American Convention Against Terrorism in June 2002. The Convention, among other measures, improves regional cooperation against terrorism, commits parties to sign and ratify U.N. anti-terrorism instruments and take actions against the financing of terrorism, and denies safe haven to suspected terrorists. President Bush submitted the Convention to the Senate on November 12, 2002, for its advice and consent, and the treaty was referred to the Senate Foreign Relations Committee (Treaty Doc. 107-18). In the 109th Congress, the committee formally reported the treaty on July 28, 2005 (Senate Exec. Rept. 109-3), and on October 7, 2005, the Senate agreed to the resolution of advice and consent. The United States deposited its instruments of ratification for the Convention on November 15, 2005.

---

[75] See the website of the CICTE available at http://www.cicte.oas.org/Rev/en/

[76] See the documents of the eleventh regular session of the CICTE, including the declaration, available at http://www.cicte.oas.org/Rev/EN/Meetings/Sessions/11/Default.asp

Legislative Initiatives and Oversight

111th Congress

In the 111th Congress, President Obama signed into law the Comprehensive Iran Sanctions, Accountability, and Disinvestment Act of 2010 (P.L. 111-195) on July 1, 2010, which included a provision making gasoline sales to Iran subject to U.S. sanctions. (Subsequently, the State Department imposed sanctions on Venezuela's state oil company, PdVSA, in May 2011 for providing cargoes of reformate, an additive used in gasoline, to Iran between December 2010 and March 2011 valued at around $50 million. See "Venezuela and Iran-Related Sanctions" above.)

Several other measures with Venezuela provisions were considered or introduced in the 111th Congress, but action was not completed on these initiatives. In June 2010, the Senate Committee on Armed Services reported S. 3454, the National Defense Authorization Act for FY2011, with a provision that would have required a report on Venezuela related to terrorism issues. In June 2009, the House approved H.R. 2410, the Foreign Relations Authorization Act for FY2010 and FY2011, with a provision in Section 1011 that would have required a report within 90 days on Iran's and Hezbollah's actions in the Western Hemisphere. On July 23, 2009, the Senate had approved its version of the National Defense Authorization Act for FY2010, S. 1390 (Levin), with a provision that would have required the Director of National Intelligence to provide a report on Venezuela's military purchases, its potential support for the FARC and Hezbollah, and other Venezuelan activities, but the final enacted measure dropped the provision.

Other resolutions and bills related to Venezuela that were introduced in the 111th Congress include H.R. 375 (Ros-Lehtinen), introduced January 9, 2009, would have, among its provisions, placed restrictions on nuclear cooperation with countries assisting the nuclear programs of Venezuela. H.R. 2475 (Ros-Lehtinen), introduced May 19, 2009, included a provision identical to that in H.R. 375 described above that would have placed restrictions on nuclear cooperation with countries assisting the nuclear programs of Venezuela. H.Res. 872 (Mack), introduced October 27, 2009, would have called on Venezuela to be designated a state sponsor of terrorism because of its alleged support of Iran, Hezbollah, and the FARC.

Over the years, the U.S. Congress has continued to express concern about progress in Argentina's investigation of the 1994 AMIA bombing, with the House often passing resolutions on the issue around the time of the anniversary of the bombing on July 18. In the 111th Congress, H.Con.Res. 156 (Ros-Lehtinen), approved July 17, 2009, again condemned the AMIA bombing and urged Western Hemisphere governments to take actions to curb the activities that support Hezbollah and other such extremist groups.

On October 27, 2009, the House Committee on Foreign Affairs, Subcommittees on the Western Hemisphere, the Middle East and South Asia, and Terrorism, Nonproliferation and Trade held a joint hearing on "Iran in the Western Hemisphere" featuring private witnesses.[77]

---

[77] A transcript and webcast of the hearing is available at http://foreignaffairs house.gov/hearing_notice.asp?id=1127

112th Congress

In the 112th Congress, several legislative initiatives have been introduced related to terrorism issues in the Western Hemisphere associated with Mexico, Venezuela, and the activities of Iran and Hezbollah in the Western Hemisphere, and several hearings have been held related to these topics.

Mexico

H.R. 1270 (McCaul), introduced March 30, 2011, would direct the Secretary of State to designate as foreign terrorist organizations six Mexican drug cartels.

H.R. 3401 (Mack), the Enhanced Border Security Act, introduced November 10, 2011, and ordered reported by the House Subcommittee on the Western Hemisphere, Committee on Foreign Affairs, on December 15, 2011, would require the Secretary of State within 90 days to submit a detailed counterinsurgency strategy "to combat the terrorist insurgency in Mexico waged by transnational criminal organizations." Supporters of the measure argue that terrorist and insurgent tactics are being employed by drug traffickers and criminal organizations in Mexico and constitute a threat to democracy. They argue that the Mérida Initiative is failing to address the problem, and that the United States needs to use appropriate counterinsurgency tactics to combat these criminal organizations. Opponents of the measure argue that Mexico is not facing a "terrorist insurgency" by groups with political goals, but is combating narco-criminal organizations that employ brutal tactics to sustain their money-making goals. They contend that the bill's call for a counterinsurgency strategy would undermine the strong security relationship with Mexico developed under the Mérida Initiative.[78]

The State Department's 2010 terrorism report, issued in August 2011, stated that "no known international terrorist organization had an operational presence in Mexico and no terrorist group targeted U.S. interests and personnel in or from Mexican territory." As noted above, the report also stated that "there was no evidence of ties between Mexican criminal organizations and terrorist groups, nor that the criminal organizations had aims of political or territorial control, aside from seeking to protect and expand the impunity with which they conduct their criminal activity."

Several hearings to date in the 112th Congress have focused on the drug trafficking situation in Mexico and allegations that the drug trafficking organizations constitute a criminal insurgency or have links to terrorism. The House Committee on Foreign Affairs, Subcommittee on the Western Hemisphere, held a September 13, 2011, hearing entitled "Has Mérida Evolved? Part One: The Evolution of Drug Cartels and the Threat to Mexico's Governance" featuring private witnesses.[79] The Western Hemisphere Subcommittee followed up on October 4, 2011, with a joint hearing with the House Committee on Homeland Security, Subcommittee on Oversight, Investigations, and Management, entitled "Mérida Part Two: Insurgency and Terrorism in Mexico," with

---

[78] "House Foreign Affairs Subcommittee on Western Hemisphere Holds Markup on H.R. 3401 and H.R. 2542," *CQ Congressional Transcripts*, December 15, 2011.

[79] A transcript and webcast of the hearing is available at http://foreignaffairs.house.gov/hearing_notice.asp?id=1348

testimony from the State Department, the Drug Enforcement Administration, and the Department of Homeland Security.[80]

Looking more broadly at drug trafficking, the House Committee on Foreign Affairs, Subcommittee on Oversight and Investigations, held an October 12, 2011, hearing entitled "The International Exploitation of Drug Wars and What We Can Do About It" featuring private witnesses.[81] The House Committee on Foreign Affairs, Subcommittee on Terrorism, Nonproliferation and Trade also held two hearings on "Narcoterrorism and the Long Reach of U.S. Law Enforcement," on October 12 and November 17, 2011, that examined the links between drug trafficking and terrorism worldwide and featured private witnesses and an official from the Drug Enforcement Administration.[82]

For further background on Mexico, see CRS Report R41576, *Mexico's Drug Trafficking Organizations: Source and Scope of the Rising Violence*, by June S. Beittel; CRS Report R41349, *U.S.-Mexican Security Cooperation: The Mérida Initiative and Beyond* , by Clare Ribando Seelke and Kristin M. Finklea; and CRS Report RL32724, *Mexico: Issues for Congress*, by Clare Ribando Seelke.

Venezuela

H.Res. 247 (Mack), introduced May 4, 2011, would condemn Venezuela "for its state-sponsored support of international terrorist groups" and call "on the Secretary of State to designate Venezuela as a state sponsor of terrorism" for "its support of Iran, Hezbollah, and the Revolutionary Armed Forces of Colombia (FARC)."

On June 24, 2011, a joint hearing on "Venezuela's Sanctionable Activities" by subcommittees of the House Committee on Foreign Affairs and the House Committee on Oversight and Government Reform featured testimony by State Department and Treasury Department officials. State Department officials expressed concern about "Venezuela's relations with Iran, its support for the FARC, [and] its lackluster cooperation on counterterrorism."[83] Administration officials testified that Hezbollah's activity in Venezuela was confined to fundraising.

For further background on Venezuela, see CRS Report R40938, *Venezuela: Issues for Congress*, by Mark P. Sullivan.

---

[80] Testimony and a webcast of the joint hearing is available at http://homeland house.gov/hearing/joint-subcommittee-hearing-m%C3%A9rida-part-two-insurgency-and-terrorism-mexico

[81] A transcript and webcast of the hearing is available at http://foreignaffairs house.gov/hearing_notice.asp?id=1365

[82] A transcript and webcast of the October 12, 2001, hearing is available at http://foreignaffairs.house.gov/hearing_notice.asp?id=1362; a webcast of the November 17, 2011, hearing is available at http://foreignaffairs house.gov/hearing_notice.asp?id=1379

[83] Joint Hearing on "Venezuela's Sanctionable Activities," House Committee on Foreign Affairs, Subcommittee on the Western Hemisphere and Subcommittee on the Middle East and South Asia, and House Committee on Oversight and Government Reform, Subcommittee on National Security, Homeland Defense and Foreign Operations. June 24, 2011. Testimony and webcast of the joint hearing is available at http://oversight.house.gov/index.php?option=com_content&view=article&id=1349%3A6-24-11-qvenezuelas-sanctionable-activityq&catid=17&Itemid=25

Iran and Hezbollah in the Western Hemisphere

Broader than the focus on Iran and Venezuela, **H.Res. 429** (Duncan), introduced October 11, 2011, would express the sense of the House that "there exists significant cause for concern and further investigation of potential counterterrorism threats from Iran's growing presence and influence in the Western Hemisphere." The resolution calls for the Administration to include the Western Hemisphere in its 2012 National Strategy for Counterterrorism's Area of Focus, with specific attention on the "counterterrorism threat to the homeland emanating from Iran's growing presence and activity in the Western Hemisphere."

In the second session of the 112th Congress, **H.R. 3783** (Duncan), introduced January 18, would require the Administration to develop "a strategy to address Iran's growing hostile presence and activity in the Western Hemisphere." On March 1, 2012, the House Foreign Affairs Committee's Subcommittee on Terrorism, Nonproliferation, and Trade approved the measure after it initially approved an amendment in the nature of a substitute offered by Representative Duncan, the bill's sponsor.[84] As amended by the subcommittee, the bill would state that it shall be U.S. policy "to use appropriate elements of national power to counter Iran's growing hostile presence and activity in the Western Hemisphere by working together with United States allies and partners in the region to mutually deter threats to our interests by the Government of Iran." The toned-down language of the amended version differs from the original version, which would have stated that "it shall be the policy of the United States to use *all elements* of national power to counter Iran's growing presence and hostile activity in the Western Hemisphere." As approved by the subcommittee, the bill would also require the Secretary of State to conduct an assessment within 180 days of the threats to the United States posed by "Iran's growing hostile presence and activity in the Western Hemisphere" and a strategy to address these threats.

Several hearings have been held in the 112th Congress dealing with concerns about Iran and Hezbollah in Latin America. In the first session, the House Committee on Homeland Security, Subcommittee on Counterterrorism and Intelligence held a July 7, 2011, hearing on "Hezbollah in Latin America—Implications for U.S. Policy," featuring private witnesses.[85] The joint June 24, 2011, hearing by the House Committees on Foreign Affairs and on Oversight and Government Reform on "Venezuela's Sanctionable Activities" cited above also touched on concerns about Iran and Hezbollah in the Western Hemisphere. The House Foreign Affairs Committee held a broader hearing on October 13, 2011, entitled "Emerging Threats and Security in the Western Hemisphere: Next Steps for U.S. Policy," with witnesses from the Departments of State, Treasury, and Defense that touched on concerns about Iran and Hezbollah in the Western Hemisphere.[86]

In the second session, hearings were held in both houses. The House Foreign Affairs Committee held a February 2, 2012, hearing focusing on Iranian President Ahmadinejad's January 2012 trip to Latin America.[87] The Senate Foreign Relations Committee's Subcommittee on Western

---

[84] See the amended language of H.R. 3783, available from the House Committee on Foreign Affairs at: http://foreignaffairs.house.gov/112/ANS%20DUNCSC_040_xml%202%2029%2012.pdf

[85] U.S. Congress, House Committee on Homeland Security, Subcommittee on Counterterrorism and Intelligence, "Hezbollah in Latin America—Implications for U.S. Homeland Security," July 7, 2011. Testimony and webcast available at http://homeland.house.gov/hearing/subcommittee-hearing-hezbollah-latin-america-implications-us-homeland-security

[86] A transcript and webcast of the hearing is available at: http://foreignaffairs.house.gov/hearing_notice.asp?id=1361

[87] A webcast of the hearing is available at: http://foreignaffairs.house.gov/hearing_notice.asp?id=1396

Hemisphere, Peace Corps, and Global Narcotics Affairs held a February 16, 2012, hearing on Iran's influence and activity in Latin America.[88]

Conclusion

For most countries in Latin America and the Caribbean, threats emanating from terrorism are low. Terrorism in the region is largely perpetrated by groups in Colombia and by the remnants of radical leftist Andean groups. According to the Department of State, most governments in the region have good records of cooperation with the United States on anti-terrorism issues, although progress in the region on improving counterterrorism capabilities is limited by several factors, including corruption, weak governmental institutions, weak or non-existent legislation, and reluctance to allocate sufficient resources. Both Cuba and Venezuela are on the State Department's list of countries determined to be not cooperating fully with U.S. antiterrorism efforts, and Cuba has remained on the State Department's list of state sponsors of terrorism since 1982. U.S. officials and some Members of Congress have expressed concern over the past several years about Venezuela's relations with Iran, with concerns centered on efforts by Iran to circumvent U.N. and U.S. sanctions and on Iran's ties to Hezbollah, alleged to be linked to two bombings in Argentina in the 1990s. There is disagreement, however, over the extent and significance of Iran's activities in Latin America. The State Department maintains that there are no known operational cells of either Al Qaeda or Hezbollah-related groups in the hemisphere, although it notes that ideological sympathizers continue to provide financial and moral support to these and other terrorist groups in the Middle East and South Asia.

Author Contact Information

Mark P. Sullivan
Specialist in Latin American Affairs
msullivan@crs.loc.gov, 7-7689

---

[88] Testimony and a webcast of the hearing is available at: http://www.foreign.senate.gov/hearings/irans-influence-and-activity-in-latin-america

---